ISBN 978-0-656-73532-7
PIBN 11336623

1 MONTH OF
FREE
READING

at

www.ForgottenBooks.com

By purchasing this book you are eligible for one month membership to ForgottenBooks.com, giving you unlimited access to our entire collection of over 1,000,000 titles via our web site and mobile apps.

To claim your free month visit:

www.forgottenbooks.com/free1336623

CANADA:

ITS GROWTH AND PROSPECTS.

TWO LECTURES

DELIVERED BEFORE THE MECHANICS' INSTITUTE,

TORONTO,

ON THE 13TH AND 27TH FEBRUARY, 1852.

BY THE REV. ADAM LILLIE.

SECOND EDITION OF THREE THOUSAND EACH.

Toronto:

THOMAS MACLEAR, 45, YONGE STREET.

PRINTED AT THE GUARDIAN STEAM POWER PRESS.

1852.

ITS GROWTH AND PROSPECTS,

TWO LECTURES

DELIVERED BEFORE THE MECHANICS' INSTITUTE,

TORONTO.

ON THE 13th AND 27th FEBRUARY, 1852,

BY THE REV. ADAM LILLIE.

SECOND EDITION OF THREE THOUSAND EACH.

Toronto:

THOMAS MACLEAR, 45, YONGE STREET.

PRINTED AT THE GUARDIAN STEAM POWER PRESS.

1852

73429

PREFATORY REMARKS.

"THE GROWTH AND PROSPECTS OF CANADA" is a subject of so great importance, of so universal interest, so little understood and so much misunderstood, that we are happy to have an opportunity of re-printing from the *Journal of Education for Upper Canada* for March, 1852, the very able lectures of the Rev. ADAM LILLIE lately delivered before the Mechanics' Institute of the City of Toronto. Mr. LILLIE's talents and industry admirably qualify him for the statistical investigations which he has undertaken and pursued with so much fairness and so great labour, and we may add, with so satisfactory, and to many unexpected, results.

It is below the impulses of a generous and noble mind to seek to depreciate the character, and institutions and progress of a neighbouring community, whether of a city, a church, or a country; and we are persuaded every true hearted Canadian will cordially respond to the remark of the eloquent MACAULAY, in reference to the people of the United States:—"It is scarcely possible that an Englishman of sensibility and imagination should look without pleasure and national pride on the vigorous and splendid youth of a great people, whose veins are filled with our blood, whose minds are nourished with our literature, and on whom is entailed the rich inheritance of our civilization, our freedom and our glory." (*Miscellaneous Writings—Review of Southey's Colloquies on Society.*) But it must indicate impulses less generous and noble to depreciate the character, the institutions, the progress of one's own country.

Too much of this spirit has been indulged in Canada, to the great injury of our social contentment and public happiness. One of the most formidable obstacles with which the Department of Public Instruction has had to contend; has been the impression and assertion that Canada was too far behind the neighbouring States to adopt such a system; and the arguments to the reverse have often been received with great distrust, and sometimetimes with absolute incredulity. Mr. LILLIE's Lectures is the first attempt by a general examination and comparison of statistics, to remove the erroneous and injurious impression which has long and extensively prevailed, as to the comparative progress of Canada and the United States. By this inquiry, we think Mr. LILLIE has rendered an important service to his adopted country. We are sure every American will admit the candour and diligence with which Mr. LILLIE has prosecuted his inquiries, while every Canadian must rejoice at the conclusions which these inquiries have established—conclusions which should excite in the mind of every inhabitant of Canada increased respect and love for his country, and prompt him to labour with more confidence and energy than ever for its advancement and prosperity.

The present edition has been most carefully revised and corrected; and some slight additions have been made to it.

FIRST LECTURE.

LADIES AND GENTLEMEN,—The subject to which I am, this evening, to call your attention,—interesting in itself from its relation to the progress of our race and the providence of God,—must to us have a special interest, because of its reference to ourselves. My theme is the growth and prospects of Canada—in other words, the advancement we are ourselves making, with the anticipations we may cherish for ourselves and our children.

By the excellent lectures delivered by Mr. ROBERTSON, in the early part of the season, on the history of Canada, I am happily relieved from the necessity of occupying your time with preliminary details. Hence, with your permission, I will proceed at once to the topic announced, only premising that I speak chiefly, though not exclusively, of Canada West. This I do partly because I am better acquainted with it and have the materials relating to it more within my reach, partly because it is newer than Canada East, partly too because I think the comparisons so often made between the two sides of the Line fair only when confined to Upper Canada.

The population of Canada at the time of its surrender to Britain in 1760 is variously stated at 60,000 and 69,275, exclusive of Indians. Of these estimates, the former is that given by the Board of Registration and Statistics, which I extract from one of Mr. Scobie's very valuable Almanacs (that for 1850) ;* the latter that supplied by Mr. Smith, (in his excellent work on which I have taken the liberty of drawing freely)† from the report of Governor Murray.

With the exception of a few trading stations, of which Kingston and Detroit were the chief, this population was confined to the lower

---

* Scobie's Canadian Almanac and Repository of Useful Knowledge, for the year 1850, containing Statistical, Astronomical, Departmental, Ecclesiastical, Educational, Financial and General Information. 8vo, pp. 80. Published annually. Toronto: H. Scobie.

† Canada, Past, Present, and Future : being a Historical, Geographical and Statistical account of Canada West, containing 10 County Maps and one General Map, with a Business Directory. By W. H. Smith, author of the Canadian Gazetteer. Royal 8vo., vol. I., pp. cxxiv, 290, 80, & 24 = 518. Toronto: Thomas Maclear, Publisher.

part of the Province; nearly the whole of its upper portion being then a wilderness, occupied by the Red Man as a hunting ground. From 1770, parties, chiefly old soldiers, began to come in from the other side: to which some considerable additions were made after the Declaration of the Independence of the United States by United Empire Loyalists from New Jersey and Pennsylvania, who located themselves along the frontier Townships. So late, however, as 1791, the date of the Constitutional Act, the whole population of Upper Canada is declared to have been "calculated at less than 50,000." According to the authority already quoted (that of the Board of Registration and Statistics) it amounted in 1811, twenty years after the separation of the Provinces, to only 77,000. Hence it is not more than forty years since its growth can be said to have commenced, if so much as that.

From that time it has, with occasional interruptions, advanced steadily, and, especially during the last twenty-five or thirty years, at a rapid rate. Bouchette reports the population to have been in 1824—151,097; which, taking as he does, 77,000 as the number in 1811, makes it nearly double in thirteen years.—(Vol. I. p. 108.)

If for the sake of securing all possible exactness we connect with the above Mr. Smith's statement of the numbers in 1814 (95,000) and 1825 (158,027) respectively, the rate of increase, though somewhat reduced, is still 67 or 68 per cent in eleven years.

Between 1824, (from which period the calculations agree) and 1834, a rise takes place from 151,097 to 320,693; which is doubling in ten years, with 18,499 over. The next fourteen years bring us up from 320,693, to 791,000—the return for 1850. Within the brief space of a quarter of a century there is an advance from 151,097 to 791,000; which gives us at the close of that period over five times our population at its beginning—more than ten times our population in 1811, or according to Smith, close upon ten times that of 1806.

Lower Canada, during the same time, rose from 423,630, to 791,000; the same number with the Upper Province; being an increase of nearly 90 per cent.

Taking Canada as a whole its population has increased from 60,000 to 1,582,000 in 90 years. Hence in 1850 it was over 26 times what it was in 1760; more considerably than 2½ times what it was in 1825, when it numbered 581,657.

"All this," exclaims Haman (Est. v. 13), at the close of a glowing description of the height to which he had been elevated and the glory with which he felt himself encircled, " all this availeth me nothing, so long as Mordecai the Jew sitteth at the king's gate." What "availeth" it, some of us peevishly exclaim, that we are growing at a rate which cannot be denied to be rapid, so long as our neighbours on the other side of the Line are so far outstripping us ? How far do you conceive, are they outstripping us ? Let us look at the facts, however terrible they may prove to be. Wise men hold it well in very bad cases to know the worst.

Compare we then Upper Canada, first with the free States of the Union, then with the State of New York, and lastly with Ohio, Michigan, and Illinois conjoined; and see what the result will be.

According to the American Almanac for 1851, page 212, and "The World's Progress" (a "Dictionary of Dates" published by Putnam of New York in 1851) page 481, the Free population of the United States, was, in 1800, 5,305,925. The latter work, (Appendix, p. 704) states it to amount to 20,250,000 in 1851. In 1810 it was 7,239,814, (page 481.)

Thus it is in 1850 about (not quite) four times what it was at the commencement of the century ; while Upper Canada contains, as we have seen, over ten times the population it possessed in 1811 ; or, at the lowest calculation, ten times its amount in 1806. The slow growth therefore turns out to be a rate of progress not much under thrice that of our neighbours who are supposed to be moving ahead of us so fast. Slow growth this of rather an anomolous description. Taking the ten years between 1840 and 1850, the difference is less : though during that time we have advanced at a rate fully twice that of the Free States, whose increase has been 45 per cent. (that of the whole States being 33½ ; World's Progress, p. 704), while ours has been 94 or 95 per cent.

In Lower Canada the increase for the thirteen years between 1831 and 1844 was nearly 35 per cent—to wit 34.94 (Scobie's Almanac 1850, p. 53.) An increase of fifty per cent. has taken place within the last seven years in the county of Quebec ; which has advanced from 12,800 in 1844, to 19,074 in 1851.

Let us turn now to the State of New York, one of the best in the Union. That State contained in

1810,	-	-	-	-	959,049 Inhabitants.
1820,	-	-	-	-	1,372,812 do.
1840,	-	-	-	-	2,428,921 do.
1850,	-	-	-	-	3,200,000 do.

[World's Progress, pp. 443, 704.]

In 1850 its population is thus 3½ times (a trifle over) what it was forty years before, that of Upper Canada being in the same year close upon 8½ times what Smith makes it in 1814 ; or over ten times its amount in 1811, as stated by the Board of Registration.

Not amiss this, we should think, for a country of whose *slow growth* so much is heard.

It is, however, towards the West the tide is flowing. Let us pass with it, and mark the results.

For the purpose of comparison we have chosen the States of Ohio, Michigan, and Illinois combined, chiefly for these two reasons; first, because they have been, we believe, among the most rapid in their growth—sufficiently rapid at all events to make the comparison fair for the West ; and secondly, because our statistics enable us to take in a longer period than we could have done in the case of some other States which we should else have been disposed to include.

Availing ourselves once more of the aid of our old friend "The World's Progress," we ascertain the united population of these three States to have been in 1810, 247,570—viz. Ohio, 230,760 ; Michigan, 4,528 ; and Illinois, 12,282. They stand as follows in 1850—Ohio, 2,200,000; Michigan, 305,000 ; and Illinois, 1,000,000.; in all 3,505,000, or fourteen one-sixth times their numbers, forty years before. This assuredly is a splendid increase; enough, and more than enough to justify the most glowing of the descriptions we hear of what the West is destined to become.

How will poor Canada West stand in comparison now ? Let us see.

As already observed the Board of Registration and statistics gives the population of Upper Canada as 77,000 in 1811. Between that and 1850, when it is set down at 791,000, there intervenes a period of 39 years, within which we have an advance of close upon thirteen times (twelve six-sevenths) to set over against fourteen one-sixth times in 40 years. Does not this bring them sufficiently near to prevent their despising one another; to make them regard one another with respect and interest ?

Here, it will be observed, the statement of the Board of Registration is followed. Should it be objected that Mr. Smith makes the numbers larger in the earlier period, being unwilling to question the accuracy of that gentleman, who has evidently taken great pains to inform himself, and produced a work eminently reliable—

thereby laying the community under an obligation, of which, I trust, they will show their appreciation in the proper way ;—I know only one satisfactory method of disposing of the difficulty, namely, to take as the basis of comparison a period at which the representations substantially coincide.

For 1810 then let us substitute 1830, which will allow twenty years for development and comparison. In that year Ohio, Michigan and Illinois contained in all 1,126,851 inhabitants : Ohio numbering 937,637 ; Michigan 31,639, and Illinois 157,575. Hence the number in 1850 (3,505,000) was three and one-fifth or one-sixth times that of 1830.

Canada West contained in 1830, 210,437. Twenty years after, namely in 1850 (1849, Smith) it numbers, as we have seen, 791,- 000—over three and three-fourth times what it did in the former year ; which makes the scale descend handsomely in our favour.

Thus it turns out that Canada West is advancing at a rate fully equal to that of the best of the Western States.

These comparisons, triumphantly as it has come out of them, can hardly be denied to be unfair to Upper Canada, or at all events to stretch fairness to its utmost limit ; because they set selected portions of the States against her as a whole, and because the Western States are growing, to the extent of the native portion of the immigration, at the expense of the others. Of the increase of the Western States a large portion consists not of additions to the country as a whole, but of mere removals from one part of it to another ; while the increase shown to have taken place in Canada West, is an increase on the whole. The difference which this fact makes in the calculations will be illustrated immediately, though already it can hardly fail to have been observed from the disproportion in the rate of growth above exhibited between the newer States and the Union as a whole.

There are one or two remarks of a general nature which I would first make in relation to the States in the West.

Their most rapid increase takes place usually during the earlier periods. To no inconsiderable extent it springs from the wish to obtain possession of the lands at the original Government prices. As soon as the prospect presents itself of an early sale of these, often before they are surveyed, a rush is made upon them. By and by, the best portion of the lands being taken up, while numbers, large numbers it may be, still come in, the *crowd* moves in another direction ; or waits in anticipation of the early opening of some newer territory. · At this moment parties are passing on from the older to the newer portions even of Iowa, while others are looking with desire mingled with hope to the vast regions on the Missouri River, still in the hands of the Indians.

How far our friends on the other side are gainers on the whole by these unlimited · facilities for the obtaining of new lands may admit of a question. From what I observed in the West last summer during a journey of 3,200 miles through Michigan, Illinois, Missouri and Iowa, I should doubt the immediateness, at all events, of the gain. The issue will by and by perhaps be good ; and *that* is a great deal—the grand point indeed so far as the race is concerned—but this spreading out so largely involves now, I am disposed to think, no small amount of unnecessary hardship ; holds civilization, for the time being, at a lower level than it would otherwise reach ; and tasks the church and the nation to supply to the extent needed, the means of Christian and general instruction ; though in the latter case it may be chiefly the agents that are wanted from abroad, as an appropriation for schools is generally made in these newer regions, at an early period, if not from the very first.

Let us look now for a moment or two at the effect of comparisons of selected portions, that the severity of the test to which Canada has been subjected may be seen.

Take, by way of experiment, the Home District*—(we use the old name for greater convenience)—setting it over against the States selected.

That District contained in

1799,	-	-	-	-	224 Inhabitants.
1824,	-	--	-	-	16,609 · do.
1834,	-	-	-	-	46,288 do.
1842,	-	-	-	-	83,301 do.
1850,	-	-	-	-	· 113,607 do.

Here we have an increase in 51 years of more than 500 times ; while Ohio, whose population amounted in 1800 to 45,365, shows in fifty years an increase of between 48 and 49 times. To be sure by carrying it back ten years farther—to 1790 when it numbered 3000—it is brought up in 1850 to over 730 times ; but this only increases the advantage of the Home District, which in the year in question contained none at all.

---

* In 1852, the United Counties of York, Ontario, and Peel—the metropolitan Counties of Upper Canada, containing, according to Bouchette, 1,361,600 acres.

The population of Indiana was in 1850, when it numbered 1,000,-000—177¼ times what it was in 1800 (5,641); but this it will be perceived is greatly under the Home District within the same time.

Here we see how conclusions drawn from particular cases may mislead when applied generally.

While in Upper Canada there have been differences in rate of growth, yet the comparative rate is hardly less satisfactory than the amount on the whole, the different sections having generally maintained a fair proportion to one another.

The Gore and Wellington Districts (formerly one) present us, for instance, with an increase of more than 19 times in 33 years; having advanced between 1817 and 1850 from 6,684 to 130,661. Within the same period the Western District has risen from 4,158 to 31,199—an increase of over seventimes; London from 8,907 to 46,805—between five and six times increase; Norfolk County from 3,137 to 17,504—between five and six times; Niagara District from 12,540 to 46,543—nearly four times; while in seven years Oxford has nearly doubled, having increased between 1841 and 1848 from 15,621 to 29,219.

The following extract from a statement furnished by the Clerk of the Peace to the Board of Registration, and Statistics, shows the extraordinary progress of the Huron District in a period of 9 years:

The population of the Huron District, (now the United Counties of Huron, Perth and Bruce) in 1841 was 5,600.
In 1847, six years thereafter . . . . . 16,641.   Increase, 11,043
In 1848, one year thereafter . . . . . 20,450.   Increase, 3,807
In 1850, two years thereafter . . . . . 26,933.   Increase, 6,483

The last quotation is nearly independent of the new and fast settling county of Bruce, which, owing to the infancy of its municipal institutions, only returned 360 persons for the townships of Huron and Kincardine, but which may now confidently be assumed to contain from 3,000 to 4,000 inhabitants—say 3,067—or a total population of the three united counties of 30,000
Being an increase for 1849 and 1850 of 9,550
Or a total increase, since 1841, of 24,400
an increase almost incredible, as by reference to Smith's work on Canada, it will be found that the Huron District has made more rapid progress since its first settlement in 1827, than Lower Canada did in one hundred and four years, its population then being (in 1721) 24,511.

---

* By the census of 1852 just taken, the population is 37,480, which shows that in the short space of two years the increase has been 10,547.

Well, it may perchance be said, it would seem all is right, thus far ; for we have not merely been increasing in numbers as rapidly as our neighbours when we had supposed our growth slow compared with theirs ; but more rapidly, much more rapidly : what however is to become of us in the future ? The immense European immigration pouring in annually to the States, will certainly in a short time turn the tables completely against us. This is another popular fallacy. In spite of all we have heard on this topic, or may have joined in saying on it, the balance here too is in our favour, largely in our favour. We receive, in proportion to our numbers, a much larger share of immigration than our neighbours.

"The World's Progress" (p. 309) sets down the immigration from Europe, during the year ending 30th September, 1848, at 218,-453. For the year ending June 30th, 1849, it amounted to 299,610 ; (Ibid. 698.) Since that it has risen, I believe, to something over 300,000. The immigration into Canada amounted in 1845 to 25,-375 ; in 1846, including 2,864 from the United States, it reached 35,617 ; being exclusive of these—32,753.

For the sake of comparison reckon that for the States 300,000 ; and that for Canada 30,000 : this will come, we presume, on both sides, very near the fact.

Throwing the slaves out of the calculation, the population of the States is to that of Canada about as fifteen to one ; while the addition made to it by immigration, instead of being (what it would require to be to equal our increase from the same source,) as *fifteen* is only as *ten* to one.

Thus is our assertion demonstrated that here too the balance is in our favour, largely in our favour.

In the *Globe* of last Saturday,* as doubtless many now present have observed, the fact which I have just stated was shown in regard to the immigration from the British Islands. You will perceive it holds in relation to the *entire immigration.* Though I had made my calculations before I saw that article, the confirmation it afforded of the conclusions I had reached, (for which, I confess, I had hardly been prepared,) gratified me much. My notice of this matter will be excused, as I would not like to seem to take a good idea even from a newspaper without acknowledgment, the gentlemen of the press having the same right which others have to the credit of their own productions.

---

* 7th February, 1852.

. In Davis's "Half Century" (Boston 1851) the immigration into the United States between 1830 and 1850, is estimated (p. 29) at 1,500,000, or over. Scobie's Almanac for 1848 (p. 54), reports 466,179 as the Canadian immigration for the 18 years between 1829 and 1846 inclusive. For the two deficient years add a tenth, 46,618—the number for the twenty will amount to 512,797. Between our population and that of the States the discrepancy was much greater during the period in question than it is now. Call the proportions, however, the same then as now (in doing which we relinquish a very large advantage) our immigration compared with that of our neighbours is more than five to one. Theirs, instead of fifteen which their population requires, is only three to our one—hardly that.

On this topic we would merely add that the immigration to Canada for 1851, was up to 11th Oct., 40,299 (Canada Directory, p. 581.)*

As illustrating the success which has attended settlement in Canada West, I would mention that in the eight years, from 1844 to 1850, inclusive, £92,655 4s. were remitted through the Canada Company alone by emigrants to their friends in the British Isles and Germany, to bring them out to this Province; according to the published statement of the Company, the number and amount of these remittances were as follows, viz.:—

NUMBER.	AMOUNT.	YEARS.
549	£4,611 10 11	1844.
790	7,532 10 2	1845.
1,101	9,744 3 5	1846.
2,081	15,742 13 11	1847.
1,839	12,547 8 5	1848.
1,798	12,575 13 7	1849.
2,454	14,385 6 9	1850.
2,621	15,515 16 10	1851.
13,233	£92,655 4 0	

Be it observed I am not depreciating the United States. For running them down the facts brought out furnish no room. Did they, however, do so, I would scorn to use them for such a purpose. The

---

* The Canada Directory: containing the names of the professional and business men of every description in the cities, towns, and principal villages of Canada : together with a complete Post Office Directory of the Province ; a Directory to Public Offices, Officers, and Institutions ; and a variety of statistical and commercial Tables, exhibiting the Population, Trade, Revenue, Expenditure, Imports, Exports, Public Works, &c., &c., of Canada, and a variety of other useful information, brought down to November, 1851; By Robert W. S. Mackay. Royal 8vo., pp. 692. Montreal : John Lovell.

man who can seek to elevate himself, or that which is *his*, at another's expense, I despise. Moreover, he who thus acts pays himself, his friends, his country, a very poor compliment. I wish simply to show that taking what is recognized on all hands as the very beau ideal of progress—an example of it hardly, if at all, to be paralleled—*we* are progressing at a rate which should, not merely, stifle complaint, but inspire the warmest gratitude and the brightest hope. In what I am doing I consider myself but as giving God, our Helper, the source and sustainer of the progress described, "the glory due unto his name."

Hitherto I have dealt exclusively with the increase of our population, that which, in connection with its character, forms the basis of National prosperity. Let us now direct our attention to the increase which has been going on, at the same time, in the quantities of land under cultivation, in agricultural and other products, in stock, and in the property represented by the Assessment Rolls, with the rise in the value of Land.

The Western District (Counties of Essex, Kent and Lambton,—contents 1,616,640 acres) contained:—

In 1842,	- -	69,355	Acres of Land under cultivation.
1844,	- -	82,726	do.	do.
1848,	- -	115,708	do.	do.
1850,	- -	425,279	Acres were occupied. How much

cultivated, I cannot say.

In the London District, (Counties of Middlesex and Elgin,—contents 999,040 acres) the quantities under cultivation were:—

In 1842,	-	-	-	-	112,633	Acres.
1844,	-	-	-	-	130,329	do.
1848,	-	-	-	-	177,752	do.

The Brock District (County of Oxford—contents 584,320 acres) stands as follows :—

In 1842,	-	-	-	-	67,397	Acres cultivated.
1844,	-	-	-	-	83,046	do.
1849,	-	-	-	-	125,741	do.

We find in the Gore District (Counties of Halton, Wentworth, and Brant—741,761 acres):

In 1842,	-	-	-	222,098	Acres under cultivation.
1844,	-	-	-	266,848	do.	do.
1848,	-	-	-	310,513	do.	do.

The Home District (Counties of York, Ontario and Peel—contents 1,361,600 acres) shows the following returns:—

In 1801,	-	-	-	-	4,281 Acres cultivated.
1811,	-	-	-	-	14,578 do. do.
1821,	-	-	-	-	39,732 do. do.
1831,	-	-	-	-	101,290 do. do.
1841,	-	-	-	-	253,708 do. do.
1848,	-	-	-	-	376,909 do. do.

By way of specimen of the increase of products between 1842 and 1848, we select two or three items. The former of these years yielded, in Upper Canada, 2,321,991 bushels of wheat ; 478,117 of oats ; 3,699,859 lbs. maple sugar ; 1,302,510 lbs. of wool : the latter, 7,558,773 bushels of wheat—an increase as compared with the former year of 4,336,782 bushels ; 7,055,730 bushels of oats—being an increase of 2,267,563 bushels; 3,764,243 lbs. maple sugar—an increase of 64,384 lbs; with 2,339,756 lbs. of Wool— a quantity exceeding that of the former year by 1,037,246 lbs.

To illustrate the increase in stock, we give (Smith, vol, i. p. 122) the returns for Upper Canada of horses, milch cows and oxen for the years 1825, 1835, 1845, and 1847. These are :—

	HORSES.	MILCH COWS.	OXEN.
In 1825, - - -	22,589	51,216	23,900
1835, - - -	47,724	109,606	46,066
1845, - - -	98,598	199,537	65,127
1847, - - -	113,812	218,653	72,017

A table is given in Scobie's Almanac for 1850, of the crops of the United States for the years 1840 and 1847 ; from which it appears that in proportion to population, we are much before our neighbours as to quantity of agricultural products, with the exception of rye and maize, in which, especially the latter, they greatly exceed us. There were produced for each inhabitant in the first of the years compared—4.96 bushels of wheat in the States; in Canada —6.62 : in the States—7.21 Oats ; 9.85 in Canada. Canada yielded 16.62 bushels of potatoes, while the yield of the States was only 6.35. For the second year (1847) the quantities stand:— the States—wheat, 5.50 bushels ; oats, 8.09; potatoes, 4.86. Canada, 10.45 wheat ; 9.75 oats ; 6.57 potatoes.

The assessed value of property in Upper Canada was:—

In 1825,	-	-	-	-	£2,256,874	7	8
1835,	-	-	-	-	3,880,994	13	6
1845,	-	-	-	-	7,778,917	9	6
1847,		-	-	-	8,567,001	1	0

Of these returns it is to be observed that they show only the relative increase of value ; and not, except about the earliest period, its true amount.

The difference between the real and the assessed value, about the times compared, will be illustrated by the following extract from a letter addressed by James Scott Howard, the intelligent and respected Treasurer of the County of York (late Home District), to William Gamble, Esq., Chairman of Finance Committee, bearing date, Treasurer's Office, County of York, January 30, 1850 : which confirms at the same time the view already given of the progress of that District.

"In 1801," that letter says, "the population was only 942 ; in 1848, it had increased to 83,000 ! Making an average increase in the 47 years, of 1,746, or a total of 82,058 ! The cultivated land in the same year was supposed to be but 4,281 acres, while in 1848, it had reached to 376,909 acres. The assessed value of property in 1801, would amount to £12,555 ; but in 1848, it amounted to £1,105,396, The great increase in the value of land, is strongly illustrative of the progress made. When the assessment law of 1819 was passed, the legislature estimated cultivated lands, on an average, at 20 shillings, per acre, and uncultivated at four shillings ; in 1848, the people themselves valued the former at £5 15s. 5d. per acre, and the latter at £3 3s. 3d.,—nearly five hundred per cent. advance on cultivated, and nearly 1,500 per cent. on uncultivated. But to show in addition the rapid progress, it is only necessarry to take one example out of many, and that is, that the entire taxes of the now populous and wealthy townships of Whitby and Pickering, in 1801, amounted together only to £3 0s. 3d, while in 1848, the former paid £864 15s. 5d., and the latter £695 18s. 3d.,—making altogether £1,560 13s. 8d."

The letter from which the above is taken, is accompanied by a set of tables, which show, on an estimate, excluding a considerable number of items in consequence of want of information—"Real property to the amount of £4,992,236 ; Personal property £1,206,-487, and the products of 1848, £517,359 ; making a grand total of six millions, seven hundred and sixteen thousand, six hundred and eighty-two pounds."—[Minutes of the Municipal Council of the County of York, 1850.]

The general correctness of the above estimate is corroborated by the returns of the aggregate value of the assessed property of the County in 1851, made by the several Township Clerks ; which show a total of £5,865,627—the particulars of which are given in the Minutes of Council for 1851.

The rise described in **Mr.** Howard's letter as having taken place on the price of land in the Home District, may, we conceive, be taken as not far from the average rise throughout the Upper Province—the greater portion of it at least. For example, in Oxford, wild land cost in 1795, 2s. 6d. per acre ; in 1817, 12s. 6d.; in 1850, £1 10s. to £2 10s. Its price in the Township of Townsend (Norfolk County) was, in 1796, 1s. 3d. per acre ; in 1817, 7s. 6d.; in 1850, £2 12s.: cleared land £5 6s. In Pelham (Niagara District), uncleared land brought in 1790, 1s. 3d.; in 1817, £2 ; in 1850, £3, per acre ; cleared £6.

In particular sections of the country, prices range much above those just named. Uncleared lands on the road between Brantford and Paris, which were purchased in 1834 at one pound per acre, could hardly be obtained now under £7 10s., if even at that price. In this District there are Townships where they would run quite as high ; and we believe it to be the same in other parts of the country.

We have seen that the returns of the Township Clerks for 1851 rate the property of the County of York at considerably over five times the estimate for 1848. During the three intervening years, an actual increase had of course taken place ; though to what extent it may not be easy to say. It can hardly be supposed to have been such as to reduce the difference between the real and assessed values (as formerly calculated) to much under five times. Suppose four times to be about the difference obtaining through the country generally, that would make the value represented by the returns for Canada West in 1847, £34,268,004 4s. Lest I should have made the difference too great, throw in a year, and reckon the above as a fair approximation to the actual value for 1848. Is not this a fair amount of property (though certain descriptions are not included in the estimates) to be distributed among 791,000 individuals, old and young ? It allows for each, children as well as adults, an average of £43 1s. 4½d. Can the country which is in the possession of this be justly held to be very poor ?

Convert the above sum into dollars and cents, it makes $137,072,016 80 cents. "Well," say you, "what of that ?" You shall see.

Whether the real and assessed values correspond as nearly in the State of New York as they now do in Upper Canada, I cannot say ; but suppose them to do, and assuming the calculation given above to make a fair approximation to correctness, the not disagreeable fact is brought out that, in proportion to our population, we are not much poorer than our neighbours of the Empire State.

According to the American Almanac for 1851 (p. 237), the value of the taxable property of the State of New York for 1848, was $666,089,526: something less than five times ours, with a population over four times ; including also, be it remembered, the wealth of the City of New York.

While these calculations are not given as *certainly* representing the facts to which they relate, but rather as suggesting an interesting subject of enquiry ; we may claim to have been at least as philosophically and as profitably employed in making them as in grumbling over our poverty, real or supposed, compared with our neighbours on the other side of the Lake.

The contrast which Canada West presents now to the published descriptions of it by travellers of comparatively recent date, is remarkable indeed.

Talbot states (vol. i., p. 110) that when Col. Talbot commenced his settlement in 1802, "there was not a single christian habitation within forty miles of his ... residence." This city, (then York) he describes, after 1818, as being the most westerly town in the Upper Province ; and asserts that between this and Amherstburg, a distance of 325 miles, few villages, and those few of a diminutive size, are to be met with. Dundas, Ancaster, and Burford, he declares to be the only places which, from the multitude of their inhabitants, bear the least resemblance to villages ; and the whole population of the three together, he represents as "not exceeding 600 souls." (Vol. i., p. 120.) Thirty years before the time of his writing (he published in 1824), "there was not," he says, "a single human habitation between York (this city) and the French settlements on the St. Clair, excepting the widely scattered and undisturbed retreats of the numerous Indian tribes, most of whom," he adds, "have since retired to more remote regions." (Vol. i., p. 121.)

Dr. Howison, the third edition of whose sketches bears date 1825, in describing a journey which he took from the Talbot Road to the head of Lake Erie, mentions (p. 199) that his road lay through what were then called the *Long Woods*, where there was a stretch of 37 miles of uninterrupted forest with only one house within the whole distance ; just such a solitary trip as I had myself the pleasure of making last summer in Iowa, with the exception that the solitude consists there of prairie, instead of forest.

These wildernesses are now filled with towns and villages—many of them of considerable size and beauty ; and numbers of them wealthy. Let us look at a few of them.

The site of this large and handsome city, was, in 1793, occupied by a single Indian Wigwam (Talbot, vol. i., 100) : inhabited as would appear from Bouchette (vol. i., p. 89), by two families of Mississaugas. A few years ago I had the pleasure of dining with an old farmer on the Don, who told me that he built, I forget whether the first or second house in it. The lot, on King Street of course, was given him for nothing, on condition of building on it; and he might have had as many as he pleased on the same terms. The Government House was at that time a tent ; erected, I believe, in the ravine East of the present site of the Parliament Buildings. Having been an old Loyalist Volunteer, my friend received his supplies of flour from the Commissariat, there being then none to be had anywhere else. He had the choice of the whole neighbourhood, including the present site of greater part of the city, as a farm ; but he selected the bank of the Don, three miles from this, on account of its being better land—a choice which will not surprise any one if the description given by Talbot makes any approach to the truth. His account, which we quote as a curiosity, is as follows :—

"The situation of the town is very unhealthy ; for it stands on a piece of low marshy land, which is better calculated for a frog-pond, or beaver meadow, than for the residence of human beings. The inhabitants are, on this account, much subject, particularly in spring and autumn, to agues and intermittent fevers ; and probably five-sevenths of the people are annually affected with these complaints. He who first fixed upon this spot as the site of the capital of Upper Canada, whatever predeliction he may have had for the roaring of frogs, or for the effluvia arising from stagnated waters or putrid vegetables, can certainly have had no great regard for preserving the lives of his Majesty's subjects. The town of York possesses one great advantage, which is that of a good but defenceless harbour."— (Vol. i. p. 102.)

It was in 1794 (Bouchette, vol. i. p. 89) that the ground was fixed on and the Government Buildings commenced. The population of the city was :—

In 1801	336	1817	1,200	1826	1677
1830	2,860	1832	4,000	1842	15,336
1845	19,706	1850	25,166	It is now, 1852, 30,-763.

According to the census returns for last year, the assessed value of property in the City of Toronto was £3,116,400. The annual value at 6 per cent. amounts to £186,983 5s., on which there is a taxation of £17,429.

Goods imported at the Port of Toronto during the year 1851:—

For duty,	£656,552	3	8
Free,	38,045	3	7
Total duties collected,	94,330	5	8
Exports to United States Ports,	81,841	19	8

No precise account was kept of the Exports from Toronto to Montreal, Quebec, or the Ports on Lake Ontario and the River St.

Lawrence, but it may be safely estimated at four times the amount of those to the United States, or £327,364.

Sixteen daily, semi-weekly, weekly and monthly newspapers and periodicals, are now published in Toronto, devoted specially to the promotion of Religion, Education, Medical Science, Literature and Politics.

From Talbot's description of the city I will select a few items which will assist you in forming some idea of the improvement that has taken place.

" It contains," he says, " 1336 inhabitants, and about 250 houses, many of which exhibit a very neat appearance. The public buildings are a Protestant Episcopal Church, a Roman Catholic Chapel, a Pr sbyterian and a Methodist Meeting house, the Hospital, the Parliament House, and the residence of the Lieutenant Governor."

" The Episcopal Church is a plain timber building of tolerable size, with a small steeple of the same material. It has an extensive burial-ground, which is tastefully fenced and planted."

" The Roman Catholic Chapel, which is not yet completed, is a brick edifice, and intended to be very magnificent."

" The York Hospital is the most extensive public building in the Province, and its external appearance is very respectable."

Speaking of the streets, which he describes as " regularly laid out, intersecting each other at right angles;" he states that " only one of them is yet completely built, and, in wet weather, the unfinished streets are if possible, muddier and dirtier than those of Kingston."

How changed the picture now. Into any extended description of the difference I cannot enter, which, to do it justice, would require a lecture for itself. With the Hospital, which still stands, compare the splendid Provincial Lunatic Asylum. Look at the elegant Cathedral, close by, which occupies the site of the " plain timber Episcopal Church, with its small steeple of the same material." Pass up the street and cast your eyes on the Roman Catholic Cathedral—to which no one would hold the epithet " magnificent" to be misapplied, with its chaste Bishop's Palace by its side. Walk a few steps further, and look at the noble buildings in course of erection for the Provincial Normal and Model Schools—which are not less creditable to the country, as indicating something of the feeling with which education is regarded, and to the architects and contractors of whose skill they afford such a favourable specimen—than ornamental to the city. From the Normal School return to Saint Lawrence Hall, and tell me how many handsomer structures you have seen in your travels. Step on through King Street, with its splendid stores, and Yonge and Wellington Streets, with their beautiful Banks and Mercantile establishments. Call one of the numerous cabs' which offer their accommodation, and treat yourself to a sight of the beautiful churches and other public buildings ; Trinity College and the University grounds and building, with our villas on every hand, and tell me where, on the old continent or the new, you will find a city, which, for its age, excels what was so lately muddy Little York.

Toronto is, however, but a specimen of what is going on throughout the country. Hamilton, for example, which was laid out in 1813, and contained in 1836 only 2,846 inhabitants, had grown by 1846 to 6,832, and numbered in 1850, 10,248. By the census just completed it is brought up to 14,199. It had in 1850 thirteen churches, was lighted with gas, had four foundries, with manufactories of various sorts, several banks or bank agencies, a large number of wholesale establishments, with a multitude of handsome buildings, public and private, and an extensive trade. The annual value of assessed property in the City of Hamilton, in 1851, (being but six per cent. on the estimated value of property in the city) was £94,259 8s. The duties collected there in 1850, amounted to £59,398 12s. 2d.

Dundas, the neighbour of Hamilton, distant from it only five miles—one of the three places described by Talbot as numbering 600 souls among them—had in 1845 a population of 1,700, in 1850 2,500 ; and it now contains 3,519. It had in 1850 seven churches, three flouring mills—one of them with six run of stones ;—a paper mill ; a large foundry ; an axe factory ; a woolen factory, the proprietor of which (Mr. Patterson) had the honour of taking a prize at the world's fair for blankets—as had also Mr. Gamble, of Pine Grove, Vaughan,—with other factories of one sort and another, too numerous to mention ; several. bank agencies ; many handsome buildings, public and private ; and though last, not least, a newspaper.

Brantford was surrendered by the Indians and surveyed in 1830. In 1844 its population was somewhere near 500. The census of 1850 gives it as 3,200. Now it is 4,000. Its increase during the last ten years has been nearly 300 per cent. It has seven churches ; a brick town hall and market house, which cost £2,200 ; a brick school house, erected at an expense of £700 ; with two foundries ; four grist mills ; a stone-ware manufactory ; three bank agencies ; two newspapers, with many large stores and handsome dwelling houses.

Within seven miles of Brantford stands Paris, which, from a population somewhere near 300 in 1834, had grown in 1850 to 1810, with six churches ; five resident ministers ; two-flouring mills, with seven run of stones; two plaster mills; a woollen factory; two foundries ; a tannery ; a planing machine ; a soap and candle factory ; a saw mill ; a bath brick manufactory ; a bank agency and newspaper; with private residences, in regard to which it is not too much to say that they are worthy of the eminently beautiful sites they occupy. The present population, as shown by the census just taken, is 1905—to which it has risen from 761 since 1844.

Woodstock, which was surveyed in 1833, contained in 1850, 1,200 inhabitants, with six churches ; several mills ; manufactories of various sorts, and a goodly number of fine houses—not a few of them brick.

Ingersoll, situated a few miles from Woodstock, has increased about one hundred and forty per cent. during the last four years, having in that time advanced from 500 to 1,212.

London; surveyed in 1826, contained in 1850, 5,124 inhabitants ; twelve churches, of which three were brick ; several bank-agencies and insurance companies; three foundries ; with other works of various sorts, among them a large coach factory ; three newspapers ; a brick school house (in which I saw last autumn, close on 600 scholars), erected at a cost of £1,700. Of the handsomeness of its buildings I need say nothing, for this is recognized by all who visit it. The census just taken shows a population of 7,173.

Turning aside a little from the road by which we have been leading you, we come on Galt, a beautiful town, which from 1,000 inhabitants in 1845, had risen in 1850 to 2,200 ; with six churches ; two bank agencies ; two newspapers ; a paper mill, and numerous manufactories. Within three miles of Galt is Preston, a thriving town, containing a population of 1,150.

Seventeen miles North East from Galt, stands the town of Guelph, of which the survey was commenced only in 1827, and whose population, numbering 700 in 1843, reached in 1850, 1,860. This handsome town contained in the latter year seven churches ; 2 bank agencies; several insurance offices ; three grist mills ; a saw mill ; a carding and fulling mill ; a foundry ; a woollen factory ; four tanneries ; a grammar school, a library and reading room, and two newspapers.

The town of Stratford contained in 1840 only about a dozen houses—it has now a population of 1,000.

The town of Goderich, which 22 years ago was in the midst of an unsurveyed wilderness, 60 miles from any settlement, now contains a population of 1,329.

Niagara, reported by Howison (p. 74) to contain 700 or 800 inhabitants, has now got 3,400 ; while Saint Catherines, of which he speaks (p. 148) as a "village presenting no claim to notice," has, according to the recent census, a population of 4,369.

According to Talbot (vol. i. p. 58) Quebec contained in 1816, 14,880 inhabitants. Its population in 1850 was 37,365. It is now over 40,000. Montreal, which now numbers 57,718, contained in the same year (1816) 16,000. Cornwall is described by him as containing 200 ; its population in 1850 was 1,506. Prescott he sets down at 150 ; now it is 2,156. Brockville is represented by this same writer to contain 450 souls. Its dwellings, he describes as built of wood, and tastefully painted. It had then " no church" though it possessed a parsonage-house. These wooden buildings have long ago given place to elegant stone structures, which testify at once to the wealth and taste of their proprietors. It contained in 1850 a population of 2,757, with six churches—several of them stone.

Kingston, described by Talbot (vol. i., p. 98), as the largest town in the Upper Province, contained when he wrote, 2,336 inhabitants. Its population in 1850, amounted, after various mishaps, to 10,097. It is now 14,725; and is, besides, though the dark colour of the stone of which its buildings are erected gives them a somewhat sombre aspect, a very handsome city. Its market house is a noble structure. It has eleven churches, several of them beautiful, and is the seat of a university—that of Queen's College ;—and of a Roman Catholic college (Regiopolis) and cathedral.

"Between Kingston and York" (Toronto), Talbot says, "there are two or three very small villages, the largest of which is Belleville, containing about 150 inhabitants." In 1850, Belleville contained a population of 3,500 ; and Cobourg and Port Hope—the two villages, I presume, which he thought too small and insignificant to name—the former 3,700, with seven churches, a college (Victoria, which is rendering important service, especially to that region of country), with an attendance of 60 students, 2 grammar schools, and a cloth factory, "employing about 175 hands, and turning out 800 yards of goods, per day ; and the latter (Port Hope), 2,200, with four churches, three bank agencies, several insurance societies, and a weekly newspaper.

Since Talbot's time a number of new towns have sprung into

existence between the cities named, of which we can notice only Bowmanville, laid out about 1832, which contained in 1850, 1,750 inhabitants, with eight churches, two bank agencies, a weekly newspaper, with four grist mills,—the proprietor of one of which, Mr. Simpson, obtained a prize at the world's fair for a barrel of flour ; —saw and oatmeal mills, a cloth factory, three tanneries, and two potteries.

To compare any of our cities, as to growth, with cities of such world-wide repute as Boston or New York, may perhaps be deemed somewhat too bold. As this, however, is an adventurous age, it may be worth while, were it but to prove we are not behind the times, to run the hazard.

Begin we then with Boston —New England's noble capital—which taken all in all, is without question one of the finest cities in the world. Boston contained :—

In 1790, 18,038 inhabitants.	In 1830, 61,391 inhabitants.
1810, 33,250 "	1840, 93,000 "
1820, 43,298 "	1850, 135,000 "

(World's Progress, pp. 212, 694.)

Dividing the above into two periods of thirty years each, Boston contains at the close of the first, about two and a half times its number of inhabitants at the commencement ; while the close of the second shows three and one-tenth times the number of the beginning. The population of 1850 is 8 times, or nearly, that of 1790 : Toronto being in 1850 over six times what it was eighteen years before, to wit, in 1832 ; more than 75 times what it was 49 years before, or in 1801. Between 1840 and 1850, the increase is—on Boston, 45 per cent ; on Toronto, 95. The recent census makes the increase between 1842 and 1852—100 per cent.

New York, the emporium of the New World,—a city that, for its age, will, we suppose, vie with any on earth—numbered :

In 1790, 23,131 inhabitants.	In 1840, 312,710 inhabitants.
1810, 96,373 "	1850, 517,000 "
1830, 202,548 "	

[World's Progress, pp. 444, 701·

Its increase thus stands as compared with Toronto, two and a half times in the twenty years between 1830 to 1850, against six times in the eighteen years between 1832 and 1850, or nearly eight times in the twenty years between 1832 and 1852 ; sixteen times in sixty years against seventy-five in forty-nine ; sixty-six per cent. between 1840 and 1850, against ninety-five.

Hamilton contains now (1852) over five times its population in 1836,—an interval of only sixteen years. In 1850, Montreal contained over three times that of 1816; Quebec fully two and one-eighth times—now over two and one-third—and Sorel about four and one-half times, or 6,646 inhabitants in the place of 1500.

Perchance we may be asked how our Canadian cities compare in growth with Cincinnati, or Saint Louis? Very favourably, we reply, as the following statistics prove :—

The population of Cincinnati was in 1850,—when it reached 115,590,—about twelve times its amount in 1820, (thirty years before,) when it numbered 9,642—[World's Progress, p. 245];—while Toronto had, in the same year (1850) eighteen times its population in 1817—that is, 33 years before; and has now (1852) over twenty-five and a-half times.

Davis's "Half Century" (p. 29) reports Cincinnati at only 92,000—nearly 24,000 less than the statement we have adopted. We have given the larger number, because being professedly taken from the census of 1850, we suppose it the more correct; and because too we would do our neighbour full justice.

Saint Louis contained in 1820, 4,597 inhabitants; and in 1850, 70,000—a trifle over fifteen times the previous number. Toronto, as we have seen, had in the latter year, eighteen times its population in 1817.

During the last thirty years our growth has thus, in its rate, exceeded that of both these cities, which among those of the west hold first rank.

To the specimens already given of rise in the value of land in the rural districts, we add a few illustrative of what has been taking place in the towns and cities :

In 1840, the Government paid £19,000 for 32 acres of land in Kingston; part of a lot of 100 acres which had cost the party from whom the purchase was made £500. Bishop Macdonnell paid, in 1816, £500 for 11 acres in the same city. The front portion of the block was laid out in 1840, in quarter acre lots, which brought from £160 to £250 a-piece.

Perhaps it may be said that land in Kingston had, at the time in question, an undue value given it by the circumstance of the city's being made the seat of government. Be it so; Brantford has never been the seat of government : yet two lots in Colborne Street, which cost originally £10 for sixty-six feet, were sold last summer—the one for £25, the other £30 per foot. A lot was pointed out to me last autumn, in one of the second or third rate streets in London, for which I was told from £7 10s. to £9, could easily be got.

Quarter acre lots in Guelph, which in the year 1830 were purchased for £5, command now from £300 to £400, and in some spots even higher prices. A lot in Goderich was recently leased at the annual rent of £30, which the proprietor bought 20 years ago for £10.

Forty acres of land in this city, extending from Richmond up to Gerrard Street, were sold (how long ago I cannot say) by Hon. Mr. Crookshanks to the late Hon. Mr. McGill, for 23s. 9d. per acre; which now average in value, I presume, not less than £750 per acre. The McGill property, valued by the proprietor in 1823 at £4,000, is now supposed worth from £75,000 to £100,000. Six acre lots on Yonge Street, which cost in 1825, £75; could not be purchased now, probably, under £1000.

Between 1850 and 1852, an increase of 9,622 took place in Montreal, which makes it now more than three and a half times what it was in 1816.

Bytown is described by Bouchette (vol. i. p. 81,) as containing when he wrote (about 1830) nearly a hundred and fifty houses. Its population, reported by the late census as over 8000, is therefore now probably eight times what it was in the year above-named.

The land on which Bytown stands bought for £80, is valued by Smith in his Gazetteer at £50,000 or over.

Those who have been for any length of time acquainted with the country, must be struck with the improvement going on in the character of the houses ; the handsome frame, or brick, or stone dwelling, rapidly taking the place, in all the older localities, of the log-cabin.

The roads are likewise improving fast. For example, in the spring of 1837, I journeyed from Brantford to Hamilton in company with a friend. We had a horse which, according to the fashion of these now ancient times, we rode in turn. Night came on ere we reached Hamilton. The road was in such a state that neither of us could venture to ride. Compelled to dismount, we had for the sake of safety, to plunge on through the mud, leading our horse, and sinking deep at almost every step. Such was my exhaustion, that on reaching the friend's house whither we were going, I had to rest myself by leaning my back against the door. A macadamised road of the first class now stretches, and has long done, over the puddle through which we thus laboriously forced our way.

Twelve or fourteen years ago I travelled several times between Guelph and Hamilton. Of the character of the road it would be useless to attempt giving a description to those who have not seen it. The thought of the journey used almost to terrify me. On one of these occasions—of which the recollection is still fresh, and likely long to be—I met a friend midway; when turning aside round a large mud hole, half occupied by a great stump, we halted under the shadow of the huge pines which skirted the road; and inquired of one another's welfare, and of the " going," very much as ships meeting at sea make mutual inquiries as to longitude, latitude, course, and so forth. Not far from the time of which I speak, a minister, who had just come out from England and was going to Guelph with his family, was, by a shrewd friend who accompanied him, taken round by Brantford—a distance of 57 miles or thereabouts.—instead of proceeding direct from Hamilton (26 miles), under the idea that had the new-comers gone through the road I have mentioned, they would, on reaching their destination, have imagined themselves to have got whence there was no egress. No trick like this, which was reckoned a clever one at the time, would now be necessary; as between Hamilton and Guelph there is an excellent macadamised road. At present the journey from Toronto to the latter place, which would then have required nearly two days, is performed in about twelve or fourteen hours, and will, when the projected railway opens, be accomplished, without fatigue and at a trifling expense, in a couple of hours, perhaps less.

Ere long, the plank road, which is so fast pushing the venerable corduroy back into the woods, will have to retire before the railways with which the land is likely to be covered.

How improved is our condition in regard to the conveniences of life, compared with what it was a few years ago.

The first steamboat on the Saint Lawrence was built in 1809. It made its passage between Montreal and Quebec, for which it charged nine dollars (eight down), in thirty-six hours actual sailing, being sixty-six in all between the two ports. A second was launched in the spring of 1813, whose time was twenty-two and a-half hours. The passage is now made up in fourteen hours, or less, and down in about eleven, at a charge varying from two and a-half to three dollars. The year 1816 added two to the number of the Saint Lawrence steamers. The first Upper-Canadian steamers belong to the year 1817, when two were built, one to ply between Prescott and

Kingston, the other on the bay of Quinte. Now they cover our lakes and rivers, and every year is adding at once to their comfort and beauty. The charges too at which their accommodations are afforded, are generally speaking moderate. In 1849, their number on Canadian waters amounted to 103; with a tonnage of 16,156 tons : since which time, we presume, a considerable addition has been made to both. We are to have daily this summer, it is intimated, a through line to Montreal; and a mail line, touching at the intervening ports.

In 1792 we were blessed, it would seem, with an "*annual winter express* between Montreal and the *Upper Countries*," comprehending Niagara and Detroit. The improvement was thought very great when it came as often as once in three months. Now we have not merely the mail distributing its precious load daily through almost every part of the land, and in its remotest regions once or twice a week ; but the electric telegraph, by which we can, in a few moments, communicate with all the main parts of the country, and the leading cities on the other side of the lines. A message which I gave in last summer to the office in Chicago about 12 o'clock noon, was delivered in Montreal within two hours.

To get an idea of the post office accommodation we enjoy, it is worth your while to look into Scobie's excellent Almanac for this year, where you will find over five pages of names of offices and post-masters. For the trifling sum of three pence we can send a letter, or as many of them as may be brought within half an ounce weight, from one end of the land to the other. Nor is this all, we have a cheap book and parcel as well as letter, postage.

The mercantile progress of the country outstrips, if possible, its progress in the respects we have been contemplating. At least it fully equals it.

In 1805, 146 vessels, with a tonnage of 25,136 tons arrived at Quebec ; the vessels numbered in 1827, 619, with 152,712 tons ; while in 1849 the vessels reached 1,184, besides 144 to Montreal, in all 1248, with a tonnage of 502,513 tons. The tonnage arrived at Quebec last year amounted to 531,427—besides 230 vessels to Montreal (*Globe* 3rd Feb., 1852.) In the year 1849, the tonnage of vessels registered in the Province was 87,461 tons, nearly 3½ times the amount of the whole tonnage to the country in 1805. The vessels were 723, (Scobie's Almanac, 1851) all but five times, the number trading to the country in the year 1805. The value of the imports to Quebec was in 1850—£688,441 10s. 9d.; in 1851 —£833,929 5s. 10d.

According to an agreement made with Lower Canada in 1795, by which the Upper Province was to receive an eighth of the "duties payable on goods, wares, or merchandize, entering the Lower Province;" the share of Upper Canada amounted in 1801 to £903 currency. The customs of Upper Canada yielded in 1846, £391,-171 1s. 3d. For the United Province the duties collected in 1850 reached the sum of £615,694 13s. 8d.

Canada imported in 1850 articles to the value of £4,245,517. Its exports, during the same year, of its own domestic products, amounted to £2,669,998.—(Scobie's Almanac, 1852.) During 1850, 1250 vessels passed down the Welland Canal and 1259 up; while last year the down vessels amounted to 1752, and those going up to 1748.—(*Quebec Gazette*—Toronto *Globe*, Feb. 3rd, 1852.)

How we stand in relation to some of these points when compared with the United States, the following returns will show.

The total customs received into the Treasury of the United States for the year ending June 30th, 1849, amounted, as given by the American Almanac for 1851, to $28,346,738 82 cents—that is, between eleven and twelve times the customs of Canada (£615,694 13s. 8d—$2,462,778 74 cts.) with a population more than fifteen times ours.

The value of the products of the United States exported in 1849, was $132.666,955—(American Almanac 1851, p. 172)—less than thirteen times ours in 1850 (£2,669,998, or $10,679,-992) for a population fifteen times as large.

Between the value of the inports of the two countries for the years specified the difference is still greater, those of the States being under nine times ours—to wit—$147,857,439—against £4,245,517 or $16,982,068.

In the President's Message for last year the exports of 1850 are shown to have reached a sum considerably higher; but as the difference is described to have arisen, not from the increased quantity of products exported, but from a temporary rise in price in the earlier part of the year, it affords no fair basis for comparison.

From a table given in the American Almanac for 1851, (p. 165; see also Davis's "Half Century," p. 29) showing the exports, imports, &c. for each year between 1791 and 1849, it appears that the exports of the United States reached their highest value in 1839, when they rose to $162,092,132, being $1,892,252 over fifteen times ours (the proportion of the population) for 1850.

Small as this excess is, it is in appearance only it exists, because the sum named above includes, not as it ought to do, the products of the country merely, but the *entire exports*. The difference between the two in that year I have no means of ascertaining; but in 1849 it was $29,425,177. Suppose it to have been the half of this in 1839, an addition of thirteen millions or thereabout would be necessary to bring up the exports of the United States in their highest year to ours for 1850, the difference in population being taken into account.

It is time our remarks on the material interests of the country were brought to a close. Thanking you for your patience and courtesy, I must reserve what I have to say on its higher interests—those, namely, of a mental, spiritual, and civil character,—as also its prospects, till this night fortnight, when, with your permission, the subject will be resumed.

SECOND LECTURE.

LADIES AND GENTLEMEN:

In accordance with the intimation given at the close of last Lecture, I have to call your attention, this evening, to the progress which is being made by Canada, Canada West especially, in her higher interests, or those of a mental, spiritual and civil character ; with the prospects which are opening upon her.

Mr. Smith tells us that the number of newspapers in Canada, in 1810 was five, which were all published in the Lower Province. Kingston has now, if I am not mistaken, as many ; Hamilton has, I believe, one more ; Quebec somewhere about twice, and Montreal and Toronto each more than thrice the number. Canada West, which in that year had none, and only eight or ten when Bouchette published (vol. 1. p. 111), must, I conclude, from a list I have just seen, have over ninety—not much probably under a hundred. The whole number in the Province I cannot positively say; but judge it must be at least a hundred and fifty—or thirty to one what it was forty-two years ago.

This, I am disposed to believe, our friends on the other side would call going ahead. Ninety where within the memory of by no means "the oldest inhabitant" there were none, they would, at all events, recognise as a very creditable advance.

On few things do our neighbours pride themselves more, justly we believe, than on their newspapers. Yet, young as we are, we have nothing to fear from comparison even here.

The number of newspapers in the United States, as stated by Davis in his "Half Century" (p. 93) was 200 " as nearly as can be ascertained," in 1800; 359 in 1810; 1,000 in 1830 ; 1,400 in 1840 ; and in 1850 about 1,600. Of this last number 371 were in the New England States, and 460 in New York. The " World's Progress" (p. 445) reports 1,555 in 1839. A calculation I have lately seen reckons them now 2,800.

Taking this latter as their present number the supply would be, in proportion to population, equal to about 180 to us; or 90 to Canada West, which is rather under than over the fact.

With twenty millions of people to whom to look for subscribers provided he succeed in securing the general respect, an Editor can, of course, afford an expense for the procuring of information and the command of talent, which would otherwise be beyond his reach. Hence should individual papers be found among our neighbours excelling ours in fulness and ability, it would be but what was reasonably to be anticipated. Whether this be the case in fact, or to what extent, I cannot say ; but from the specimens I have seen on both sides, which have been somewhat numerous, I question whether ours will not, on the whole, compare favourably with theirs in character. My impression is that they will. Without pledging myself for the correctness or propriety of all their contents—which, I conceive, their conductors would not always defend on reflection—I but state the truth when I say that the amount of good writing and good thinking contained in them has often surprised me.

The number of hook-stores found in our cities and larger towns, viewed in connection with the extent of their stocks ; and the books contained in the libraries of our various institutions and met in our dwellings, would seem to indicate that a taste for reading exists : while the character of many of them shows it to be to a considerable extent correct; though, we doubt not, improvement in this particular is at once possible and desirable.

In Education—one of the first interests of a community—a progress highly satisfactory is being made, as the following particulars derived from the Chief Superintendent, the Rev. Dr. Ryerson's very valuable Report for 1850 demonstrate.*

The number of Common Schools in operation in 1846 was 2,589 ; containing 101,912 pupils, and being sustained at an expense of £67,906 19s. 1¾d. In 1850 the schools numbered 3,059, and the pupils 151,891 ; with an expenditure of £88,429,-8s. 7¼d—an increase of 470 on the schools ; 49,979—close on fifty per cent.,—on the pupils ; and, on the amount of expenditure, £20,522 9s. 5½d. Besides this, £14,189 14s. 0½d. was appropriated to the erection or repair of school-houses—an item of which, previous to 1850, no return was made. As compared with 1842 the sum available for the salaries of common school teachers

---

* Annual Report of the Normal, Model and Common Schools in Upper Canada for the year 1850 ; with an Appendix. By the Chief Superintendent of Schools. Printed by order of the Legislative Assembly. Crown 8vo., pp. 390.

was considerably more than double—being £88,429, against £41,500.

Between 1847 and 1850 the private schools have increased in a still greater ratio, having advanced from 96, with an attendance of 1,831, to 224, with 4,663 scholars—a result gratifying on a variety of accounts. The Academies and District Grammar Schools have advanced, within the same time, from 32, with 1,129 pupils, to 57, with 2,070 ; which is nearly doubling both the institutions and their attendants in the brief space of three years.

The grand total in attendance on educational institutions was in 1842, 65,978 ; in 1846, 101,912 ; and in 1850, 159,678.

Compared with previous years there is in 1850 some diminution in the number of pupils in Colleges and Universities; which will, we trust, prove only temporary, the attendance having risen between 1847 and 1849, from 700 to 773.

The following particulars, derived from the American Almanac for 1851, will assist us in forming an idea as to how we stand when compared with our neighbours, in regard to the number of our common schools and the parties being educated in them, with the sums expended in their support.

In Ohio, with a population over two and three-fourths ours, there were in 1848, 5,062 schools, with 94,436 pupils, sustained at a cost of $224,801 44 cents—or £56,200 7s. 3d.; of which $149,205 44 cts. were from public funds, and $75,596 from other sources (p. 277).

Illinois, whose population is over a fourth more than ours, had in 1848, 2,317 schools, with an attendance of 51,447 pupils, supported partly by the proceeds of a school fund and partly by tax. The amount expended for the year I could not gather from the statement given (p. 286).

Michigan with a population nearly two-thirds ours, had in 1849, 3,060 schools, containing 102,871 pupils : towards the support of which $52,305 37 cts. were paid from the School Fund, and $75,-804 92 cts. from taxation—in all $128,110 29 cts., or £32,275 1s. 5d.

Michigan had thus in 1849, in proportion to its population, about the same number of scholars we had in 1850. While, however, the number of schools was a third more than ours, in proportion to population (one more only in fact); the sum paid for their support was much under one half—a circumstance which, when we consider that our teachers are under, rather than overpaid, suggests doubt as to efficiency. With them the number of female teachers is much larger than with us, which accounts, in part, for the difference.

. With a population a fourth over ours, Illinois had in 1848, 271 fewer schools than we had in 1846, with only about half our number of pupils ; about one-third our number of pupils in 1850, with .742 fewer schools.

Ohio had in 1848, with a population two and three-fourths ours, about double our number of schools, with 7,476 less than our number of pupils in 1846; considerably under two-thirds our number in 1850. The amount paid for their support came short of ours in 1846 by £11,706 11s. 10½d.

It would thus appear that in the very important matter of Common Schools we are decidedly before the states just named, which may, we suppose, be taken as a fair specimen of those of the west generally.

The number of schools in the State of New York in 1849, was 13,971—a little more than four and one-half ours for 1850, with a population about four and one-twenty-secondth. Of pupils in attendance, the number was 778,309 ; exceeding ours, according to population, in a proportion somewhere near four and one-fifth to four and one-twenty-secondth. On the support of these schools the sum, expended was $1,115,153 62 cents, or £275,788 7s. 7½d—under three and one-fifth times ours. For our population then we have in 1850 spent a considerably larger sum on common schools than did the State of New York in 1849.

The pupils taught in private schools in New York State are supposed to amount to about 75,000 ; a number about equal to four times ours, after allowance for the difference in population. In this particular, our neighbours have largely the advantage of us.— [American Almanac, 1851, p. 236.]

Massachusetts had in 1849, 3,749 public schools, with an attendance of about 180,000 pupils (173,659 in summer—191,712 in winter); costing $336,060, or £209,015. Making allowance for the difference in population,—about a fourth more than ours;— the number of schools and pupils is nearly the same as ours for 1850—rather under than over—but in proportion to population, the sum paid for tuition is considerably (£10,000) more than double. This liberal dealing with her Teachers reflects high honour on the Bay State ; which will, we doubt not, find the money thus expended one of her best investments. Over and above her public schools, this State had in the same year (1839) 1,111 private academies and schools incorporated and unincorporated; in which 31,447 pupils were receiving instruction, at an additional cost of $302,478.

Thus are we initiated, in some measure, into the secret of the superiority of Massachusetts over her sister states; of the respect she commands every where, and of the influence she is exerting in the newer regions, whither her sons are carrying her churches and schools and modes of feeling, and where their efforts will by and by be crowned with a success which will more than reward them.

In the character of the instruction given in our schools, an improvement is taking place fully equal, we believe, to the progress making in other respects. Here the Normal School is, under the superintendence of its able and indefatigable masters, rendering us great service.

The substitution which there seems a disposition to make, wherever practicable, of large school-houses, erected on the most approved principles, and supplied with all the facilities for instruction which the best text-books, maps, plates, apparatus, and so forth afford,—but above all with such a number of qualified Teachers as admits of proper subdivision of labour and classification of pupils—in the place of the small, ill-ventilated room in which the scholars have been wont to be shut up with their single and oppressed master, is peculiarly gratifying. Schools like those in London and Brantford, which I have had the pleasure of seeing in operation, I should think it difficult for any one to visit without wishing to see the country covered with them.

As illustrative of the spirit of our schools, it is worthy of observation that, while no violence to conscience is attempted or countenanced, the Bible is read in 2,067 of them, or fully two-thirds of the whole; and that, in many cases, ministers of the gospel, of various denominations, hold, by the choice of the community, the place of superintendents.

The increase of visits paid to the schools by "clergymen, councillors, magistrates and others," which were in 1850, 18,318 against 11,675 in 1847, shows a growing interest in them which is pleasing; but the fact by which the country's feeling in respect to them is expressing itself most unequivocally, is the readiness, unanimity, and liberality with which the people are taxing themselves for their support.

For the improvements we have been tracing, so full of hope for the future, it is but justice to acknowledge that we are largely indebted to the intelligence, the singleness of purpose, and the untiring industry with which the Chief Superintendent of Schools is devoting himself to his very important avocation; in connection with the generous and enlightened liberality of the government and the community.

· In the number and extent of school libraries, we are greatly exceeded by our friends in the States ; but they are beginning to be introduced among us, and will, we hope, ere long, become universal.

Our facilities are increasing in the higher departments of education, as well as the more common. To the number of our grammar schools, considerable additions are, as we have already seen, being made ; and we have occasion to know that their general improvement, with the placing of their advantages within more easy reach of the community, is engaging the anxious attention of those, (not a few of them at all events,) entrusted with their management.

Our Provincial University, with its staff of well qualified professors, to which important additions are being made, is now too holding out a first-class education to the youth of the country, at a charge little more than nominal—a boon of which, I trust, they will show their appreciation by the extent to which they shall avail themselves of it.

· Though a denominational institution, Trinity College claims also to be mentioned here as augmenting the facilities for education in the higher departments, professional and general. Queen's and Victoria Colleges, already noticed, may again be named in this connection as increasing these facilities.

In Canada East, the Directory for 1851 (p. 554), reports, besides the high-schools of Montreal and Quebec (institutions of a high order) and certain academies in the eastern-townships: nine colleges, with an attendance of 1500 pupils—exclusive of the seminaries of Quebec and Montreal, the former of which numbers twenty-two professors, with 385 students ; the latter eighteen professors, and 250 students. Quebec has also a Historical and Montreal a Natural History Society, both excellent institutions ; to which is to be added McGill College, which possesses, we believe, university powers. A list, confessedly incomplete, is furnished in the Directory (p. 555) of Libraries in the different parts of the Province containing an aggregate of 43,296 volumes. The largest number reported in any one library is 10,000—that of the Montreal Seminary ; and the next 8000—being that of the Montreal College.

A list is given in the American Almanac for 1851 (pp. 196–199) of 121 colleges and universities, extending as to time of founding from 1636—when Harvard was instituted—to 1849 ; with four libraries containing 10,000 volumes each ; two 11,000 ; five 12,-000 ; one 14,000.; one 15,000 ; three 16,000 ; one 17,000 ; one 19,000 ; one 23,000 ; one 25,000 ; one 31,000 (Brown University) ; one (Yale) 49,000 ; and one (Harvard) 84,200. With some of these we have nothing to compare, our institutions being as yet in their infancy ; though we hope to have in time. The aggregate number of volumes in the 121 libraries is 789,967. Besides these there are libraries found in all their larger cities ; many of them of considerable extent and value. As much as ten years ago I had the pleasure of looking at one in New Bedford, Massachusetts, which contained 10,000 volumes ; and I spent a couple of hours on the evening of the 3rd of July last, in examining one in Saint Louis—the Mercantile Association Library—which, though including only about 5,000 volumes, is of the first class as to character. The books embrace almost every department of knowledge—history, civil and ecclesiastical, theology, law, medicine, science and art, poetry, biography, travels and general literature ; are admirably chosen, and many of them the best editions to be had. To the young men especially of that city they constitute a treasure of the highest order. Nor could I help cherishing pleasing hopes in regard to these young men, when I saw some of them perusing these valuable works with apparently deep interest amid the report of fire-arms and the discharge of fire-works on the eve of their grand National Festival. The high gratification the above fine library afforded me, with the courtesy shown me by the intelligent and gentlemanly librarian and other parties-present, must be my excuse if I have dwelt too long on this institution. Glad should I be to see such a collection of books open to the mercantile community of this city. And why should there not be ? With a fair measure of effort it might, in a moderate time, be secured.

In a sketch, however brief, of the intellectual progress of our country, it would be unpardonable, here especially, to omit notice of the increase in number and advance in character of our Mechanics' Institutes, which, with their libraries, and apparatus and lectures, promise soon to cover the land. If what has taken place in the case of the Institute whose members I have now the honour of addressing, may be received as a specimen of what is going on elsewhere, the country is certainly to be congratulated. Not many years ago the attendants here were indeed " few and far between." Now this commodious hall is generally filled with an audience as intelligent, attentive, and respectful as a modest man need wish to have before him.

To the notices already furnished in relation to the Educational Institutions of Lower Canada, may here be added that in 1850, there were in that portion of the Province, during the first six months, 1,879 schools, with 73,551 scholars; towards which £12,-693 had been paid out of the public school grant ; and that between 1842 and 1850 £249,530 had been paid to teachers, and £52,921 for the erection and repair of school-houses.—(Scobie's Almanac for 1852—p. 31.)

There is a particular of higher importance still than any hitherto named in which we are making a progress very marked, namely; in facilities for religious instruction and worship. Our churches and ministers are multiplying fast. In some respects the rapidity of the increase may perhaps be a disadvantage, as it has a tendency to keep the congregations smaller and weaker than they might otherwise be ; yet the earnestness of which it furnishes evidence is commendable, while it, at the same time, prepares beforehand a supply for the multitudes pouring in upon us so fast.

From a Report of a Committee of Assembly, presented 15th March, 1828, it appears there were at that time in Upper Canada, 236 ministers—about half of them Methodist,—some of whom had come in as early as 1792. The number at the commencement of 1851, as stated in the Canada Directory (p. 553) was 869—one to every 870 of the population. At this moment they can hardly be under 900. In 1828 the number of churches was 141 or from that to 150 ; 66 of them being Methodist. They are reported in 1848 to amount to 895—six times their number only 20 years before. Now they must be as many as 950, or from that to a 1,000. Rapidly as our population is growing it thus appears that the churches are increasing faster—being now six times as numerous as they were 20 years ago, while our population, as we have seen, numbered in 1850 something more than five times what it was 25 years before.

This is a fact worthy of notice as indicating the feeling of the country. Not merely, however, are the churches as to number keeping pace with, outstripping the increase of the population : but in character they are rising with the wealth of the community : becoming in proportion to that, at once, more commodious and more handsome. In their case as in that of the dwellings of the people, brick and stone are, in many parts, taking the place of wood.

The Home District in 1850, contained 163 churches. In the Gore District they had risen between 1817 and 1848, that is, in thirty-one years, from 4 to 64, exclusive of those in the Wellington, formerly included in the Gore District. Seventeen years ago Paris con-

tained none., All denominations worshipped in the school-house.
In the fall of 1834 I recollect being told by a brother minister that
he had on the Sabbath before been one of three who waited turn
for the use of the house. Now Paris contains, as has been noticed
already, six churches (one stone and one brick) with five resident
Protestant ministers. Brockville, you will recollect, had no church
when Talbot visited it. Now it contains six. Brantford, which
had none 18 years ago, now contains eight. In this city, instead of
the four which Talbot names, we have now twenty, exclusive of
four or five at Yorkville—which in his time, and much later, had
no being, its site—now occupied with so many handsome villas—
being covered with woods.

Furthermore, the organizations to which Christianity has given
birth elsewhere, such as Bible, Tract, Missionary, Temperance and
Anti-Slavery Societies ; with Sabbath Schools, and institutions for
the relief of the destitute and recovery of the sick, are found in
activeoperation among us: conferring their varied blessings on those
who need and will accept them ; besides holding a place in the
public esteem and enjoying a measure of its patronage which give
promise of growing strength and service for the future.

This city contains four Theological Institutions—to which a fifth
will probably soon be added—where a considerable number of young
men are preparing for the ministry among the different denominations.

In Lower Canada the Directory [p. 553] reports 641 clergymen ;
being one to 1,190 of the population.

All, I presume, whatever their difference of opinion in regard to
some points, will admit that during the period which has passed
under review, no small improvement has taken place in our laws,
our civil arrangements, and in the understanding and application of
the principles of government. Things are now placed to such an
extent in the hands of the people that, if they fail to move on in
harmony with their notions of propriety, they will find it difficult,
to discover parties other than themselves, on whom to throw the
blame. Our Municipal Institutions are, we believe, working well ;
on the whole—improving the country, while they are at the same,
time, by the duties to which they call them, giving the people the
consciousness of power and teaching them so to use it as to pro-
mote the general prosperity and ensure peace and general sati.fac-
tion.

Other topics will suggest themselves to you of which note
might be taken, perhaps ought to be ; but we must hasten to a close.

In the face of the facts above adduced, what is to be thought, Ladies and Gentlemen, of the depreciatory comparisons so often made between ourselves and our neighbours as to rate of progress ? They are, in my opinion, as erroneous as in their operation they are calculated to be mischievous. The impression which forced itself most strongly on my mind during the journey to which I have referred elsewhere, was the striking coincidence in appearance (with the exception of prairie in place of forest) and condition between those States and Canada West. They are progressing rapidly ; but so are we. New towns present themselves on every hand ; small, it is true, many of them ; yet destined to be large ere long. Thus too it is with us. With theirs our Towns compare very favourably ; so do our rural districts. My belief is that a Canadian farmer would return from such a tour as I made somewhat disposed to boast ; that he would say our cultivation is at least as good as that of the West ; and our farm houses as good, and provided as comfortably.

In the progress of our neighbours I rejoice ; and would be happy, instead of wishing it retarded, to see it accelerated. This would gratify me, not merely for their sake and for the sake of the world, but for our own. We have an interest in their growth, which operates as a spur and encouragement to us. To a young country like this it is an advantage which cannot easily be rated too high, to have an intelligent, energetic people along side of us, whose experience, whether successful or otherwise, we can turn to account.

The good qualities which we all recognise in our neighbours form an additional reason for the cultivation of a spirit of respect and kindness towards them. Add to this our oneness in origin, in language, and in whatever is most important in thought and feeling; and the cherishing of any other spirit will be seen to be, not a simple impropriety, but an offence, a crime. God, moreover, seems to have marked out one high and honourable destiny for us—the privilege of showing on one of the most splendid of theatres, what christianity and freedom and intelligence can do for men; and of realizing their united blessings in proportion to the fidelity with which we fulfill the trust committed to us. What is good among them let us imitate : but let us act with discrimination ; and not like children, hold their cake and rattle to be better than our own, and brawl for them, merely because they are theirs.

The time you have been already detained, forbids my dwelling on the Prospects of our noble country, however inviting the theme. My belief is that it is destined, at no distant day, to hold a high and honourable place among the nations; and to exert an influence, wide and powerful, on the world's well-being.

Of these ant'cipations we have an earnest in the progress we have been contemplating ; as we have a pledge for them in her extent and natural advantages, and in the character of her people and her institutions ; taken in connection with the correcter views beginning to be entertained in relation to her, and the apparent plans of the infinitely wise and gracious Sovereign of the universe.

A few words on some of these points, with a practical suggestion or two, and we close.

According to Bouchette (vol. i. pp. 64, 182), Canada contains an area of 346,863 square miles—Lower Canada 205,863, and Upper Canada 141,000—an extent about six times that of England and Wales. Surely here we have ample room and verge enough— space to expand till we become, so far as numbers can make us, a *mighty nation.*

The writers whom I have had opportunity of consulting, speak, with one consent, in high terms of the agricultural capabilities of our country.

Howison declares the " soil" of Upper Canada to be "in general excellent, and likewise of easy cultivation ;" (p. 247).—points out its superior adaptation to the production of fruit (246) and flowers (281); and affirms its capability, under proper culture, of yielding crops very much superior both in quantity and quality to those obtained while he was resident in it (248). The "climate" he describes as being, " in the westerly parts of the Province particularly, alike healthful and agreeable." (242). He looks also with confidence for its improvement as the land becomes cleared (242– 247). In respect to the prospects of emigrants, he expresses himself as follows :—After relating that he had " resided eight months in the most populous and extensive new settlement in the Province, and daily witnessed the increasing prosperity of thousands of people, most of whom had been forced from their native land by poverty," he continues: "No one who emigrates to Upper Canada with rational views, will be disappointed. The country is becoming more agreeable every day, and only requires a large population to render it equal, in point of beauty, comfort, and convenience, to any part of the earth. The delightful asylum which it affords to the poor and unfortunate of every class, is a circumstance that has hitherto been little known or appreciated, and one which is of particular importance at the present time, when agricultural and commercial embarrassments have reduced so many individuals to a state of destitution and misery" (272). There is much in this writer of a similar character, which we cannot quote. (See pages 214, 215, 252, 271, 278, 281, 283.)

"The climate of Upper Canada," Talbot writes, (vol. ii. pp. 157, 168) "although verging toward the extremes of heat and cold, is . . . . . . very fine, highly favourable to the growth of grain, and the production of the finest fruits ; and the soil, though badly cultivated, is not surpassed in fertility by any tract of land of equal extent on the American continent. All kinds of grain which are among the productions of the Mother Country, are cultivated here with astonishing success ; and many fruits and vegetables, which in Great Britain and Ireland are only raised at immense labour and expense, attain in Canada, without the assistance of art, a degree of perfection wholly unknown in more northern countries."

The extremes of heat and cold are less in the western peninsula of Canada than they are several degrees south of it, as proved from observations extending over a period of from 10 to 20 years, which may be seen in a Treatise on the Climate of Western Canada, by H. Y. Hind, of the Normal School, published in 1851.

"In point of salubrity," Bouchette avers in his accurate and fine-spirited work (vol. i. 349), "no climate in the world can perhaps be found to exceed that of Canada, which is not only a stranger naturally to contagious or fatal disorders, but extremely conducive to longevity. In the early periods of the settlement of the Upper Province, the fever and ague were indeed very prevalent ; but as the cause of this local affection was gradually removed by the draining of marshes in the progress of cultivation, it has almost entirely disappeared." Of the different portions of the country he speaks in terms very similar, while passing them under review.

The geological survey which has for some years been going forward under the able superintendence of Mr. Logan, is bringing to light a variety and amount of mineral wealth surpassed in few quarters of the globe. An interesting catalogue of the minerals already discovered, with their respective localities, prepared by Mr. Logan for the World's Fair,—may be seen in Scobie's Almanac for the present year, as also in the Canada Directory for 1851.

Facilities for commerce, almost unbounded, are furnished by our rivers and splendid lakes—justly termed inland seas—which will be ere long increased by our railroads already in progress, or projected, with others sure to follow them.

For a vigorous and honourable use of these advantages, and hence for the future greatness of the country, we have a guarantee in the character of our population.

We have to be sure the reputation of being deficient in enterprise. On the supposition of the truth of this charge, I should like to know how the progress we have been contemplating, of which but a very hurried and imperfect sketch has been presented, is to be accounted for. I can think of only two theories on which its explanation can be attempted—to wit, that of the celebrated David Hume, which would annihilate the handsome buildings and well-filled stores which we imagine ourselves to see around us, with the elegant steamers that seem to ply on our lakes and rivers, and the cultivated farms and barns bursting with plenty, apparently presenting themselves to our vision—and the comfortable looking people with whom we conceive ourselves to be meeting and mingling, where so lately there was nought but wilderness; and have us believe them to be all pure matters of fancy, ideas existing in our own foolish brains (though on that hypothesis even these must be unreal)'; or one on which, when a boy, I have heard the erection of the old Glasgow Cathedral explained, which has been declared to me, without if or but, to have been built by the fairies during the night. Perhaps these benevolent gentry have been and may still be at work here; and it may be to them we owe what we speak of in our ignorance and pride, as the works of our own hands.

Should these theories be repudiated, a fair measure of enterprise must, we think, be granted us. Look at the manner in which numbers of the cities and municipalities are taxing themselves for the railroads referred to above, and other improvements. Is it thus people void of enterprise are wont to act? He must be somewhat fool-hardy who will charge the citizens of Hamilton with want of enterprise, in the face of the fact that for the completion of the Great Western Raliroad they are voluntarily paying ninepence in the pound on their assessed value.

The value of enterprise to a country like this, to any country, we are disposed fully to admit. In so far as deficiency may exist, we would, therefore, counsel improvement; but we hold the representations often made on this subject, and believed, it is to be feared, by not a few from the confidence with which they are uttered, to be altogether contrary to fact; and, to parties situated as we are, most ungenerous and mischievous.

From what has been shown above, in relation to schools, churches, and the other means of christian instruction, the inference is irresistible that our people are to a gratifying extent, though by no means the extent desirable, imbued with the love of knowledge and impressed with a reverence for God.

It is true, differences of opinion exist among us, as experience shows them to have always done, though in varying degrees, wherever freedom of thought and discussion—rights most precious—

have been conceded ; but in one thing I trust we shall be found to agree, namely, in the recognition of the fact, that it is "righteousness" which "exalteth a nation," together with the determination to be governed in all things by heaven's revealed will, and to act towards one another in the spirit of the gospel which we profess in common.

But are we not slaves, prostrate on the earth, foaming with rage, and struggling to bite the foot that tramples us ? or at best held back from rebellion, with the spirit of which we are penetrated, only by the bayonets which guard us ? Would that Her Majesty's troops, if they be indeed charged with keeping us in order, found as easy work elsewhere ! Soldiering would then come as near as might be to a sinecure. It is neither force nor fear, but a love—warm as it is true—to our noble Fatherland; a respect for her character, a gratitude for her liberality, a confidence in her justice and honour; and a fulness of sympathy with her, that holds us in our present connection. Our "love makes duty light."

Here, as elsewhere, there may be something to mend, and time and patience may be required ere our institutions are perfected ; but, in the mean time, we are free, if under heaven there be such a thing as freedom. Where is the nation that can claim to take rank in this respect before us ? "Slaves cannot breathe" in Canada ; " they touch our country, and their shackles fall." Of this we have among us thousands of living witnesses; who feel themselves here to be not *things*, but *men*, and able to call the wives and children whom they love—THEIR OWN. So long as earth shall contain within her wide circumference a single slave, may Canada be ready to welcome him. not to an asylum only, but a home ; to endow him with all the rights which her own free-born sons enjoy, and know so well how to value ; to show him the sympathy to which the injured and the distressed have everywhere and at all times a right at the hand of those to whom God has given the power to aid them. Thus, we trust, it will be.

Large as the numbers are who are flocking annually to our shores, I have often wondered when looking at the advantages which Canada offers to the virtuous and the diligent, that they should not be very much larger. Such may command, almost anywhere they please to locate themselves, all the substantial comforts of life. with a very moderate measure of exertion. Who are the owners of our handsomest and best-stocked farms ? Generally speaking, men who have procured and improved them by their own labour ; many of whom you find in all the older parts of the country—living like patriarchs; surrounded by their children to whom they have given inheritances. For example, I was myself intimately acquainted a few years ago with an old gentleman thus situated in Flamborough West (where there are others in similar circumstances), whose property consisted when he came into the country of nothing more than the axe which he carried on his shoulder, with a moderate supply of clothes for himself and his young wife'; and who, ere he could procure a place where he might lie down to sleep, had to make himself a tent, by throwing a blanket over a few boughs which he cut from some of the trees in the yet unbroken forest.

Meeting some time ago with a countryman and fellow-citizen of my own, a native of Glasgow—who had occupied a respectable position at home, and whom I found living in a handsome stone house, with all the evidences of comfort around him, and in the enjoyment of the respect of his neighbours ;—I remarked to him—"I suppose you do not regret having come to Canada." "Oh no :" was his prompt reply ; "it has, to be sure, been pretty much a struggle all the time; but I have brought up seven sons, to four of whom I have given farms, and I hope by and by to be able to provide them for the rest." His time of residence in the country had been, I believe, about twenty-seven years.

No small amount of the property in our cities and towns, the mass of it might I not rather say ? belongs, as those who hear me know, to parties who have earned it by their own exertions, some in mechanical and others in mercantile pursuits. A remark made to me lately in relation to Paris, that the property in the hands of its inhabitants had been nearly all made in it, applies substantially to the entire country. Its wealth is, under God's good providence, chiefly the creation of its people—not those of other generations and the present combined—but those who occupy it now.

Generally speaking a kindliness of feeling prevails, a freedom of action is allowed provided propriety is not violated, and useful labour is regarded with a respect, which makes the country, after a time at least, very pleasant to those who seek a home in it. Few, it is well known, who have lived long in it, leave it without regret.

These various advantages, though yet to a considerable extent strangely overlooked, are beginning to be on the whole better understood. May we not hope that they will be, ere long, appreciated as they ought to be; and that we shall have increasing numbers of such as shall prove themselves useful to us while benefitting themselves, taking up their abode among us ? In the mean time let us each seek to acquit himself faithfully of the duties he owes the country ; among which we would take the liberty of specially naming—the recognition of the country's advancement and advantages ; co-operation, as far as practicable, in every prudent and honourable effort for its improvement ; with the avoidance of every thing whether in word or act, having a natural tendency to injure it.

We sometimes think our neighbours say more than enough of their growth ; but depend upon it, if they at all err here, their fault is a much less mischievous one, to say nothing else of it, than lugubrious wailing in circumstances which ought to call forth gratitude. Feeling themselves carried forward with the general movement, a buoyant and hopeful spirit is excited—which gives them strength to battle with and overcome difficulties by which they might otherwise be mastered. It would be well were such a dialogue as the following (which it is but justice to the parties to say took place at a time of some excitement), a specimen altogether unique among us. A friend of mine being gravely told sometime ago by two of his neighbours, that "Canada was no country for the farmer, who could make nothing here," turned quietly to one of them and asked : "Friend, what do you reckon your farm worth" ? "Two thousand pounds" was the ready reply. "How long have you been in the country" ? "About twenty years." "Did you bring much with you when you came" ? "No : nothing." "Then in twenty years," retorted my friend, "You have besides bringing up a family, made two thousand pounds—cleared a hundred pounds a year—and you tell me Canada is no country for the farmer." Addressing himself to the other he now enquired—"and what, my good Friend, may be the value of your farm ? Is it worth as much as your neighbour's" ? "It is worth about five hundred pounds more," the party questioned—who saw the awkward position in which his companion and himself had placed themselves —replied with a smile: "Then certainly," he was answered, "You have not done *very badly*, for you have been in the country only about the same length of time with your neighbour, and you know you have told me before you brought nothing with you."

Of the above description of poor the country contains not a small number, who reckon it little that they are in the possession of noble farms which they are every year improving, and which every year is raising in value, with stock to which they are constantly adding—so long as they may be unable to lay by, at the same time, something handsome in the way of money. To their laying by of money I have no objection. On the contrary, I should be glad to see them do it ; yet all things being taken into account, I cannot think them standing very greatly in need of pity.

In relation to the future destiny of the country a weighty responsibility rests on us all, because our conduct will infallibly have an influence upon it, for good or for evil. What we would wish to have it become in character or circumstances, let us heartily lend our aid to make it.

Let us guard with special care, amid the excitements into which an honourable zeal for what we hold to be true and right may sometimes hurry us, against the utterance of a word, the performance of an act, the cherishing even of a thought, which would excite suspicion of the country's principle, or damage its reputation, or in any way injure it. Its interests are far too sacred to be sacrificed to party feeling or party projects in any quarter or in any form. From my inmost soul I apply to it the beautiful legend of my own loved native city, "Let Canada flourish"—its older form especially—"Let Canada flourish through the Preaching of the Word."

With thanks for your attention, on which I have drawn, I fear, more largely than I ought, I bid you, Ladies and Gentlemen, Good Night,

FINIS.

JOURNAL OF EDUCATION,

Upper **Canada.**

SCIENTIA.

PUBLISHED MONTHLY,

AND DEVOTED TO

GENERAL EDUCATION, LITERATURE, SCIENCE, & ART;

THE

PROMOTION OF FREE SCHOOLS, &c.

EDITED BY

THE REVEREND EGERTON RYERSON, D. D.,

Chief Superintendent of Schools,

ASSISTED BY

MR. JOHN GEORGE HODGINS.

TERMS:—For a single copy, 5s. per annum; not less than eight copies, 4s. 4½d. each, or $7 for the eight; not less than twelve copies, 4s. 2d. each, or $10 for the twelve; twenty copies, and upwards, 3s. 9d. each. Back volumes, neatly stitched, supplied on the same terms. Single numbers, 7½d. each. All subscriptions to commence with the January number, and payment in advance must in all cases accompany the order.

Local Superintendents and Clergymen are Authorized Agents.

Toronto:

PRINTED AND PUBLISHED BY THOS. H. BENTLEY,

ALL COMMUNICATIONS ADDRESSED TO

MR. J. GEORGE HODGINS.

Education Office, Toronto.